Munshi Premchand

THE VOICE OF TRUTH

Published in 2002 by

Rupa . Co

7/16, Ansari Road, Daryaganj
New Delhi 110 002

Sales Centres:
Allahabad Bangalore Chandigarh Chennai
Dehradun Hyderabad Jaipur Kathmandu
Kolkata Ludhiana Mumbai Pune

Cover & Book Design by
Arrt Creations
45 Nehru Apts, Kalkaji, New Delhi 110 019
arrt@vsnl.com

Printed in India by
Gopsons Paper Ltd
A-14 Sector 60
Noida 201 301

Munshi Premchand

The Voice of Truth

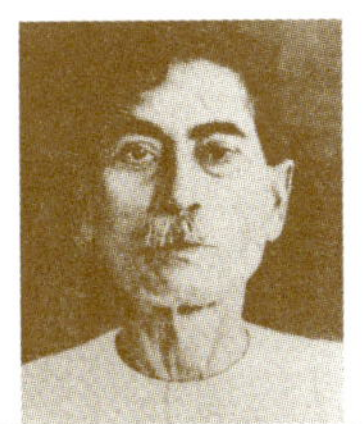

Anupa Lal

Rupa . Co

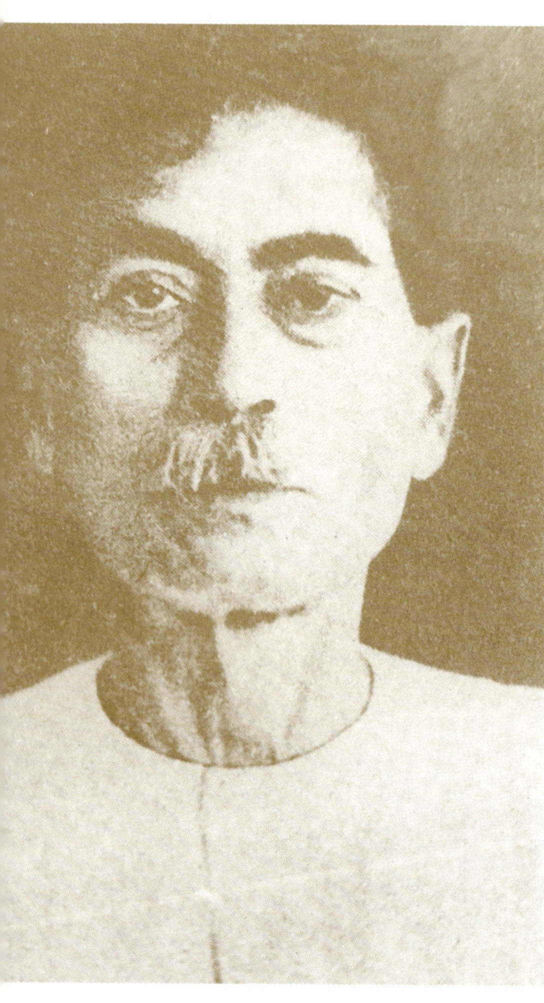

CONTENTS

Premchand

A young Urdu poet reached Lucknow to meet the well-known Urdu and Hindi writer, Munshi Premchand. At the entrance to Premchand's house, he met a man casually clad in a vest and *dhoti* and asked him for directions.

"I'll take you to Premchand," said the man. He led the young poet to a room on the first floor of the house, asked him to sit down and disappeared. He reappeared a moment later wearing a *kurta* and said with a broad smile, "Well Sir, now you are speaking to Premchand!"

On a visit to Allahabad on a hot day in May, Premchand went to meet fellow writer Mahadevi Verma. Not recognising him, the attendant at the door said loftily, "Mahadeviji is busy."

"But you have a little time, don't you?" asked Premchand, his eyes twinkling. "Come, let's sit down and talk for a few minutes."

When Mahadevi Verma emerged much later, she was horrified to find Premchand sitting under a *neem* tree in earnest conversation with the attendant, the *mali* and the *chowkidar*. He brushed aside her apologies with a laugh. "Out here I've gathered plenty of material for my stories," he said, "which you as a poetess couldn't have given me!"

This simplicity, this humour, even when he was a celebrity, were typical of Premchand. An ordinary looking man with an extraordinary talent and commitment, his name continues to be synonymous with the finest fiction in both Urdu and Hindi.

Chapter One

Early Years

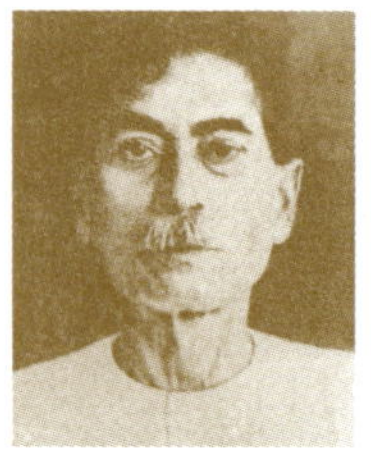

Premchand was born on July 31, 1880, in the village of Lamahi, four miles from Benaras in eastern Uttar Pradesh. By caste a *kayastha*, his father Munshi Ajaib Lal was a postal clerk — a good-natured, helpful, over-worked man of limited means, who started his career on a salary of ten rupees a month and retired when it was forty. Premchand's mother Anandi was equally good-natured and helpful. Beautiful to look at, she was known never to quarrel, gossip or backbite.

Premchand was her fourth child, born six or seven years after a

Premchand's native village-Lamahi

daughter Suggi. The first two daughters did not survive. The baby boy was named Dhanpat, master of wealth. He was also known as 'Nawab' within the family. Premchand was the pen-name he adopted many years later.

He did indeed live like a *nawab* for the first few years of his life, with the wealth of his mother's love and a carefree childhood at his command. Those were glorious days he was to recall in many a story later — raiding fields of sugarcane and green peas with his friends, blithely ignoring the shouts of angry *chowkidars*. He was an expert marksman with the catapult and could bring down any mango from a tree with a couple of expert shots. Catching fish from the village pond, to be roasted and eaten, was another favourite activity, as was playing *kabbadi*, marbles and *gulli-danda*. As he grew older he could send the *gulli* spinning a hundred and fifty yards away.

Premchand's education began when he was seven years old. He was sent to a *maulvi* in the neighbouring village of Lalpur, to learn Urdu and Persian. The *maulvi*, a tailor by profession, maintained no attendance register. Boys frequently absented themselves from class to follow their own pursuits, spending hours at the railway station, for example, watching trains come and go. The angry *maulvi* was later placated with elaborate excuses or small gifts.

So passed the days of Premchand's childhood, with a little study, plenty of play, rounded off with thrilling stories that his grandmother told the little boy at bedtime.

But tragedy struck before he was eight. Premchand's mother passed away and her going remained a wound in his heart that never healed. She had never allowed him to leave the house without putting a protective black mark on his forehead to ward off misfortune. Now he roamed barefoot, shabbily clad and

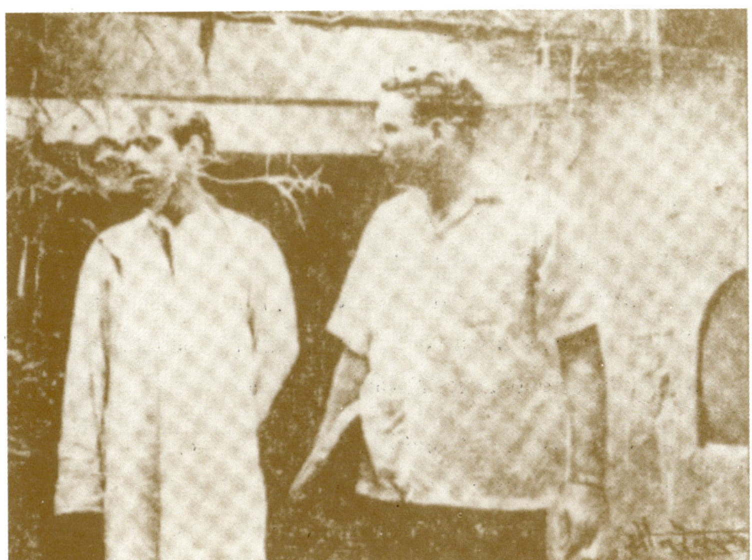

Hindi poet Trilochan with a Czech scholar at Lamahi, outside the house where Premchand was born

unsupervised. Neither his over-worked father, his loving sister Suggi who was married by then, nor his indulgent grandmother could adequately fill the gap his mother's death left in Premchand's life.

Time and again in his fiction, he returned to this early and overwhelming loss. In his novel *Karmabhumi* written forty four years later in 1932, the hero Amarkant says "The phase of a man's life when he is most in need of love is his childhood. If the sapling is watered well at this time, the roots grow strong for life. But if it is starved now, the rest of life turns arid. This was the time when I lost my mother and my soul has been starved ever since."

Munshi Ajaib Lal remarried within two years of his wife's death. With Premchand's stepmother came her young brother Vijay Bahadur, younger than Premchand and always first in her affections. The relationship between the two young boys was an amicable one, but there was no love lost between Premchand and his stepmother or *Chachi* as he always called her.

His father was posted to Gorakhpur where Premchand first went to a school named Rawat Pathshala and learnt English in addition to Urdu and Persian that he had started with the *maulvi*. Later he shifted to the Mission School in the city.

With a father too preoccupied to understand or befriend him and a stepmother for whom he was always a stepson, Premchand could easily have gone astray at that raw and impressionable age. By the time he was twelve, he was already smoking on the sly.

But something intervened to save him and give his life a direction. He developed a passion for reading and within two or three years, read hundreds of novels! Maulana Sharar, Pandit Ratan Nath Sarshar, Mirza Ruswa and Maulvi Muhammad Ali were among the leading

Premchand's Urdu handwriting

Urdu writers of that time whose tales of romance and adventure he devoured alongwith the *Tilisma Hoshruba* by Maulana Faizi, a gigantic compilation of tales of magic and suspense, said to have been written to entertain the Mughal Emperor Akbar. He read Reynold's *Mysteries of the Court of London* as well as the Sanskrit *Puranas*, in Urdu translation. Premchand borrowed all these books from a book seller-named Buddhilal. In exchange, he sold 'notes' and 'keys' to English textbooks from Buddhilal's shop to his friends in school.

Premchand's own initial literary effort was a play written at the age of thirteen. Strangely enough, it was no stirring tale of mystery or romance but the enactment of a real life incident involving a distant relative. This uncle of his had locked himself in with his low caste *chamar* maidservant in an attempt to seduce her. But the irate *chamar*community, followed by the entire village, turned up at his door. The door was taken off its hinges and the unsuccessful seducer was soundly thrashed!

Despite this humiliation he remained unrepentant. On his next visit to Premchand's home, he was as nasty and overbearing towards the boy as he had always been. But now Premchand had a weapon to wield as well as to defend himself — his pen. He wrote up the entire incident in the form of a play and read it out to his friends who enjoyed it thoroughly. He then copied out the play in an exercise book which he left under his uncle's pillow before going to school. By the time he returned, his uncle had vanished, bag and baggage. Unfortunately he took Premchand's play with him or destroyed it because it was never recovered.

After passing the eighth standard examination in Gorakhpur, Premchand had to move to a high school named Queen's College in Benaras to continue his studies. His father sent him five rupees a month for expenses but this proved to be far too inadequate.

"I had no shoes on my feet," he wrote later, recalling those days, "nor proper clothes on my body. My classes finished at three thirty in the afternoon. The Headmaster had granted me free tuition. Exams were round the corner but I still continued to give private tuition to a boy whose home I reached by 4 p.m., finishing at about 6 p.m. It was winter. My home in the village was five miles away. Even if I walked briskly I couldn't get there before eight o'clock. And the next morning I'd have to leave again at eight so as to be in college on time."

Premchand was still a student of standard nine when his father got him married. The young lad of fifteen participated enthusiastically in the festivities, only to get a rude shock when he brought his wife home and saw her face for the first time. She was fat, ugly, with a dark, pockmarked skin and she walked with a limp. Older than Premchand, she was addicted to opium, mentally not very balanced and once a month or so, seemed to be possessed by evil spirits.

The match had been arranged by Premchand's new maternal grandfather. "Your father has pushed my son into a well," Munshi Ajaib Lal said to his second wife bitterly. "Such an unspeakable wife for my handsome son."

The shock and guilt he felt may well have hastened Ajaib Lal's end. He passed away a year-and-a-half later, after a long illness. Premchand was left to fend for himself, his wife, his stepmother and her two sons. There were five mouths to feed and no income. Jobs were hard to come by and in any case, Premchand still clung to his ambition to study further and become a lawyer. He had to take the matriculation examination in 1897, but could not because of his father's long illness and subsequent death. He did appear for the exam in 1898 and passed in the second division. This meant however, that he could not pursue higher studies in Queen's College because only first divisioners were allowed free tuition. And there was no way Premchand could have paid the college fees.

He tried to obtain admission in the new Hindu College but failed in the entrance exam for Mathematics, always his bugbear.

Since he was still determined to study further, there seemed no other course for him but to improve his maths before trying once again for admission to college. Luckily he got a job as a private

No. 504
University of Allahabad.

Entrance Examination, 1899.

Roll No. 872

I certify that Dhanpat Rae
Benares Collegiate School, aged 17 years and 6 months,
passed the Entrance Examination held in the month of January, 1899,
and was placed in the Second Division.

Allahabad
The 20th February, 1899.

Registrar.

Entrance Examination certificate

tutor to the son of a lawyer for five rupees a month, which enabled him to stay on in Benaras. There was a small room above the lawyer's stables where he was allowed to stay. He furnished it with a strip of sack cloth for the floor, an oil lamp and a few utensils. He cooked some *khichdi* for himself once a day, washed up and then went to the library, ostensibly to brush up his maths. In reality, he spent most of his time reading novels.

He contributed half the salary he received towards the expenses of his household in Lamahi and tried unsuccessfully to manage for a month on the rest. He regularly borrowed money or went without food if he was too embarrassed to do so.

Life dragged on in this manner for four or five months. Premchand's sense of desperation grew. One winter evening, when all he had eaten for the last two days was one paisa worth of roasted gram, he went to a bookseller to sell off one of his maths books. As he was leaving the shop with the one rupee he had earned, a man stopped him. He turned out to be the Headmaster of a small Mission School in Chunar, a small town forty miles away from Benaras. He was looking for a teacher who was a matriculate, offering a salary of eighteen rupees a month.

Premchand jumped at the offer. As he said later, "Eighteen rupees at that time was beyond the wildest flight of my despondent imagination." He moved to Chunar within a few days. It was a quiet, little place. Shy and industrious by nature, Premchand busied himself with his work and his own studies, while Vijay Bahadur ran the house for him. Most of his salary was exhausted within the first week. For the rest of the month, the two boys lived on credit. But by and large the time in Chunar was a good time for Premchand, although it lasted less than a year.

One day, the school football team played and won a match against the local Army Eleven. One of the white soldiers kicked an Indian player in anger. Premchand saw this and his blood boiled. Heedless of the consequences, he ran onto the ground, took a flagstick and let the whites have it! The Indian players and spectators joined him enthusiastically and gave the arrogant "tommies" a good thrashing.

Never physically very robust, Premchand was "strong of heart if not of body." He refused to take injustice lying down. The school authorities were unjust to a colleague of his named Ibne Ali. Premchand openly supported his colleague. As a result, when Ibne Ali lost his job, so did Premchand.

Chapter Two

A New Beginning

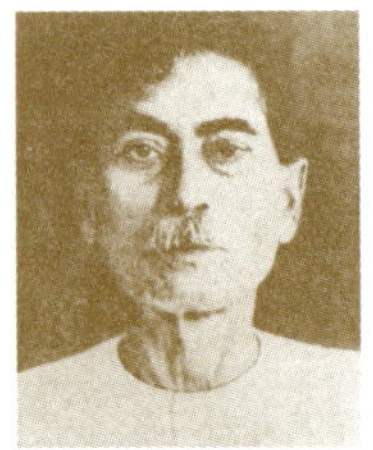

Premchand returned to Benaras and began looking for another job. With a recommendation from the Principal of Queen's College, he got the job of Fifth Master in the District School in Bahraich, with a salary of twenty rupees a month. This was the start of his twenty one years of government service.

Within two and a half months he was transferred to Partabgarh, as First Master of the District School there, on the same salary. It was hardly enough to maintain two households — his own in Partabgarh and the one in Lamahi where his wife, his stepmother and her younger son lived (her older child having died earlier).

Premchand lived in one room in the house of a *thakur,* whose two sons he tutored to augment his income. His two-year stay in Partabgarh was a fairly happy one. He was regarded as a member of the *thakur's* family, he enjoyed teaching and the climate of Partabgarh suited him. He was away from the bickerings of the two women of his household, neither of whom he cared for. And he was beginning to write regularly.

The staple fare of his reading all these years had been tales of mystery, magic and romance. But as a writer, it was not this escapist fare that interested him. It was the harsh realities of society that he saw around him — corrupt Brahmins fattening themselves on ignorance and superstition; hapless women condemned from birth to dependence, neglect and exploitation.

His idealism drew him to the reformist Arya Samaj movement which publicly at any rate, denounced social evils such as child-marriage and the dowry system and cited the Hindu scriptures in support of the remarriage of widows.

Seeing before him a lifetime of teaching and writing, Premchand decided to better his prospects by obtaining a teacher's training certificate. Granted two years' study leave, he joined the Teachers'

Training College in Allahabad in July 1902. The plainly dressed young man of simple habits and unfailing courtesy, participated fully in college activities. He joined a Laughing Club which met daily, Premchand's laughter being the loudest! But he also remained addicted to his twin passions — reading and writing.

On October 8, 1903 a novella he had written named *Asrar-e-Ma'abid* (The Secrets of the Sanctum Sanctorum) began appearing in an Urdu weekly published from Benaras. The novella exposed the licentious activities of a *mahant*, a temple priest, and his followers. Premchand's great strengths — a sharp, penetrating power of observation and the ability to tell a story so as to capture and hold the reader's interest, are already evident in this early work.

In April 1904, Premchand passed the teachers' training examination in the first division, despite his inability to teach maths. At about the same time, he also passed the special vernacular exam held by Allahabad University, in Urdu as well as Hindi, before returning to Partabgarh.

Nine months later, he was called again to Allahabad as Headmaster of the Model School attached to the Teachers' Training College. This was a great compliment for the industrious young teacher.

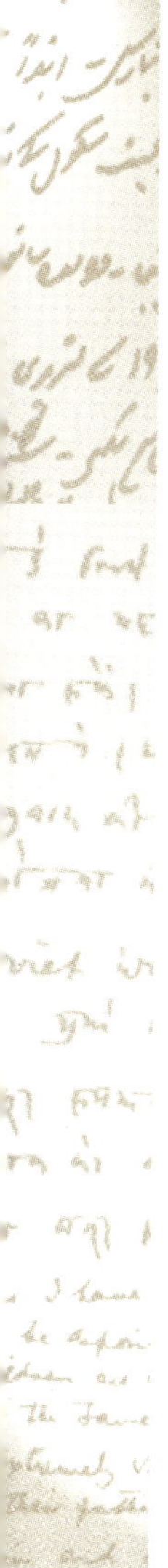

Premchand: 1907

However within three months, he was transferred to Kanpur as Eighth Master in the District School, on the same salary of twenty-five rupees a month.

Despite these upheavals, Premchand continued to write steadily. While in Partabgarh he finished his second Urdu novel *Hamkhurma-o-Hamsawab* (Together in Body and Soul) and sent it to Munshi Dayanarayan Nigam, the founder of a new journal *Zamana*, in the hope that he would find a publisher for it. The novel's hero is a young social reformer named Amritrai who, seeing the plight of young widows in Indian society, decides to marry only a widow and forsakes his beautiful and virtuous fiancee Prema.

The novel was rather contrived and contained, in Premchand's own words, "all the faults of immaturity." Even then, there are glimpses of the sure grasp of social issues and the lively, idiomatic style of narration that distinguish Premchand's best works. This novel was also published in Hindi as *Prema*.

By May 1905, Premchand had moved to Kanpur to take up his new assignment in the District School. At Munshi Dayanarayan Nigam's request Premchand stayed with him and joined his circle

Stills from Satyajit Ray's film based on Premchand's short story Sadgati.

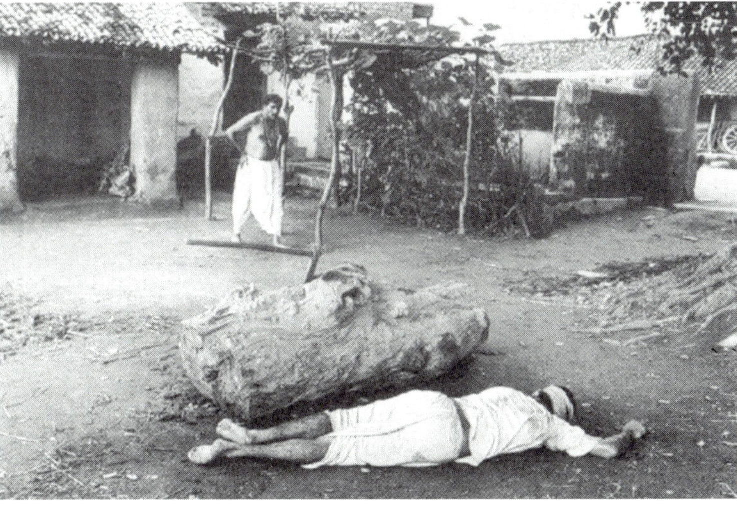

of friends and fellow writers. They met every evening to debate any and every topic under the sun. Those were heady and happy days for Premchand. Shy before strangers, he relaxed in the company of friends, recited Urdu and Persian verses, cracked jokes, laughed a great deal and made others laugh.

In glaring contrast, was the miserable and stifled existence that he led in Lamahi when he went home during his vacations. He had been married for ten years but only in name. In reality, there was no affection and no relationship between him and his wife. Frequent squabbles between her and his stepmother and a filthy, disorderly house — although it was the best one in the village — made the dreary situation even more intolerable.

That summer in 1905, the situation really became bad. One day the two women quarrelled violently and Premchand's wife tried to hang herself in the dead of night. She was prevented and the following day there was a big scene, which ended with her declaring that she wanted to go home to her parents. Premchand arranged to send her and she did not return. He did not ask her to. And that was the end of their unhappy marriage. His stepmother and her relations insisted that he remarry and found a beautiful young girl for him. Premchand was tempted. He even dreamt of his would-be wife a couple of times. As a young man of twenty-five, he yearned for the love and companionship his first marriage had never given him.

But something held him back — his conscience perhaps, or his ideals and commitment to social reform. After a lot of thought and discussion, he decided that if he were to remarry, he would marry a widow. His relatives, particularly his stepmother, strongly opposed this decision. No one in the family had ever marred a widow. What would the community say? But Premchand stuck to his guns. By chance he happened to see a newspaper advertisement placed by a Munshi Devi Prasad of Fatehpur district who wished to get his daughter, a child widow, remarried. Premchand promptly answered the advertisement.

A reply came from Munshi Devi Prasad alongwith a thirty page booklet entitled, *Redeemer* of *Kayastha Child-Widows,* written by him under a pseudonym. The views expressed were similar to Premchand's own views. He wrote back immediately asking for a photograph of Munshiji's daughter. Photographs were then relatively unknown in villages, but Munshiji had a photograph taken and sent to Premchand in Kanpur. It showed a simple, frail village girl, ordinary to look at, a little darker than him perhaps. But he was satisfied. Munshi Devi Prasad invited him to Fatehpur, approved of him and the marriage was settled. There was no question of dowry. Both sides were willing to brave disapproval and opposition from their respective communities.

On the day of Shivaratri, 1906, Premchand married Shivarani Devi. His *baraat* consisted of Munshi Dayanarayan Nigam, a few other friends and just one relative — his stepbrother Mahtab.

Premchand's life now entered a new and invigorating phase. The country too was stirring and changing as the spirit of nationalism touched the lives of more and more Indians. Swami Vivekananda's inspiring address at the Congress of World Religions in 1893 had revived the sagging self-confidence of the nation.

The Indian National Congress founded in 1885 had been toeing the official British line under the leadership of Gopal Krishna Gokhale, Dadabhai Naoroji and others. Bal Gangadhar Tilak's brand of fiery, radical patriotism clashed with this conservatism.

"The clash between Gokhale and Tilak was, among other things, a clash also between two widely different temperaments. Was the nation to attain its desired goal through revolution and rebellion and popular movement or through treaties and negotiations? Did social reform take priority or did independence?"

Premchand, with his second wife

Gopal Krishna Gokhale

"Even after accepting Tilak as his political guru, Premchand remained under the influence of Gokhale for a long time, perhaps throughout his life." Gandhi, who later made such a deep impact on Premchand, "represented an amazing amalgam of Tilak and Gokhale."

Meanwhile underground political activity gathered momentum. The first to give up their lives for India's Independence were the Chapekar brothers of Maharashtra. They were hanged by the British in 1897.

In Kanpur, Premchand kept himself very much abreast of national affairs. He regularly read several newspapers and wrote a column called *Raftar-e-Zamana* (The March of the Times), in the journal *Zamana.*

Bal Gangadhar Tilak

Zamana's editor Dayanarayan Nigam and Premchand attended the Congress session held in Ahmedabad, as observers. Premchand was a supporter of Tilak's views and Nigam of Gokhale's. The British Government began a brutal suppression of both the call for radical change led by Tilak within the Congress and revolutionary activity outside it. This alienated Premchand further. He was incensed when fifteen-year-old Khudiram Bose was hanged by the British on August 11, 1908. Although he was a government servant, Premchand put up a portrait of the brave young martyr on a wall in his home.

A year earlier he had written his first short story *Duniya Ka Sabse Anmol Ratan* (The Rarest Gem in the World). In the story this exquisite gem turned out to be "the last drop of blood shed in the cause of one's country's freedom."

Premchand himself never joined the revolutionary movement. One reason was perhaps his heavy responsibilities at home. Too many people were financially dependent on him. But he did become a "*kalam ka sipahi*," a soldier whose weapon was his pen. This soldier fought not just for political freedom, he also fought for social reform. Besides the Arya Samaj, Premchand was greatly influenced by the Social Reform League led by Gokhale and Ranade as well as by the tremendous work done by Swami Vivekananda to help and uplift the common man.

Premchand wrote many topical articles for journals like *Avaz-e-Khalq*, published from Benaras and *Adib*, published from Allahabad, besides *Zamana*. These articles included biographical sketches of Gokhale, Swami Vivekananda and the Italian freedom fighter Garibaldi. He also wrote two long stories during this period. *Roothi Rani* (The Offended Queen), emphasised the need for national unity, while *Kishna* was the story of a woman obsessed with gold. The havoc such an obsession could create was elaborated years later in his novel *Gaban* (the Embezzlement).

A collection of five of Premchand's stories of patriotism including *Duniya Ka Sabse Anmol Ratan*, was published in 1908 under the name of *Soz-e-Vatan* (Dirge of the Nation). It was well received and reviewed in Urdu as well as Hindi journals.

Editor of Zamana - Munshi Dayanarayan Nigam, Premchand's long-time friend

After four stimulating years in Kanpur, Premchand was transferred again. He was sent on promotion to a little wilderness called Mahoba, in the hilly district of Hamirpur. From being a school teacher he was now a sub-deputy inspector of schools and his salary went up to fifty rupees a month.

Just before leaving for Mahoba, Premchand had written a remarkably bold article on Primary Education in the United Provinces. Risking the displeasure of his senior officers, he had highlighted major problems such as the lack of qualified teachers, proper buildings and relevant syllabi for village schools. He had bemoaned the fact that the government spent more on inspection than on teaching.

Ironically, he was himself an inspector now. The job involved extensive travelling, on horseback or by bullock cart, often for weeks at a stretch. Premchand had plenty of opportunities to see the natural beauty of the region, to interact with its people and to listen to the local folktales and ballads.

One winter night in 1909, when he was on tour, he received urgent summons from the District Magistrate's office. Travelling over thirty miles by bullock cart, through the night, he reached there the following morning. In front of the British official lay a copy of

Premchand's book *Soz-e-Vatan*. (In those days he used to write under the name of Nawab Rai).

Khudiram Bose

"Did you write this?" demanded the Magistrate. Premchand admitted he had.

"Your stories are full of sedition!" said the Magistrate angrily. "Thank your stars you are a servant of the British Empire. Had these been Mughal times, both your hands would have been chopped off!"

Premchand was ordered to hand over all the remaining copies of *Soz-e-Vatan* and never to write anything again without the government's permission. It was easier to comply with the first order than with the second. Premchand continued to write, but no longer as Nawab Rai. 'Nawab Rai' disappeared and the pen name 'Premchand' came into existence.

CHAPTER THREE

A Writer's World

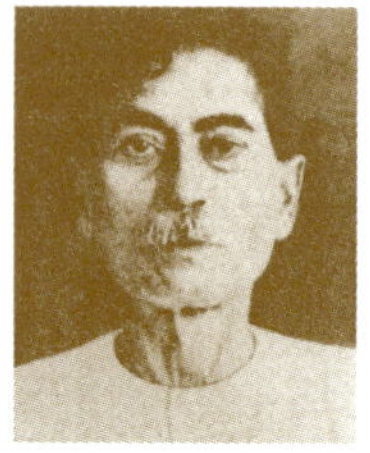

Premchand's stepmother treated Shivarani Devi no better than she had treated his first wife. Shivarani Devi was a straightforward and strong-willed woman. It irked her to see that while her mother-in-law wished to control the household, she was not really bothered about the well-being of her stepson, the sole bread-winner for the family. Gradually, as her husband wished her to do, Shivarani Devi asserted herself and the older woman started spending most of her time with her brother in Kanpur, where Premchand regularly sent her money.

The house was more peaceful and Shivarani Devi managed far better with Premchand's income than her mother-in-law had done. He was pleasantly surprised to find that she had saved a hundred and fifty rupees with which the young couple was able to buy a bullock cart for their personal outings.

In Mahoba, it was customary for officials to be supplied free milk and *ghee* by the villagers. Premchand politely declined these gifts as well as the cash he was offered when he went on tour.

Shivarani Devi gave birth to a daughter in Mahoba but the child died when she was ten months old. Two years later, another child was born and named Kamala.

Premchand's next novel *Jalwa-e-Isar* (A Spectacle of Sacrifice), was published in Urdu in 1912 and a few years later in Hindi. In this novel, for the first time he concentrated on the plight of the poverty-stricken Indian village.

"Huts with dilapidated thatches on them, walls of mud, huge heaps of rubbish in front of houses, slime-covered water buffaloes, emaciated cows... The plight of the men is truly miserable. They are mere skeletons... Not one has a whole garment on his body and each is so luckless as not even to have a square meal at the end of a day of hard toil."

Besides this novel, Premchand continued writing short stories which included inspiring tales of Rajput valour based on local folklore.

The years in Mahoba were years of comparative calm in Indian politics following Tilak's arrest. But Premchand, always a journalist as well as a story writer, felt the need to keep in touch with what was happening, nationally and internationally. He read as many newspapers as he could and wrote regularly for a few.

He had been in Mahoba for almost four years when he contracted dysentery in the summer of 1913. Despite all kinds of treatment, the dysentery gradually became chronic and Premchand grew progressively weaker. He had arrived in Mahoba as a handsome young man in his prime. Illness changed him into a prematurely old man with sunken eyes and spindly limbs. Alongwith his health, his self-confidence too went down. For a while, both his reading and writing were greatly reduced.

In July 1914, he was transferred again. He had hoped to be sent to Kanpur or at least to a healthier climate than that of Mohaba. Instead he was sent to Basti in the damp *terai* region of U.P. His salary remained the same as did his touring. Sick and despondent, he toyed as he had several times before, with the idea of giving up his government job, either to teach in a private school or to work full time for a periodical like *Zamana.* It was not so easy however, to take the plunge.

In view of his ill health Premchand managed to have his touring job changed to that of a teacher in Basti. He taught Urdu and English and was very popular with his students, regaling them with amusing anecdotes whenever he sensed their attention was wandering. The boys would roar with laughter and so would he!

One winter in Basti, it rained very heavily. And many of the mud-brick houses around Premchand's collapsed. He and his family huddled in a corner of their house for several hours, fearing a similar fate. Premchand had to miss school for a day. The following day, he had to explain his absence to the Headmaster Bhikhan Lal, who was a tyrant.

"Are you a lump of salt that you would have melted in the rain?" enquired the harsh Headmaster.

"No Sir," said Premchand, "but houses all around us were collapsing and we feared ours might too."

"Could you have prevented it from collapsing by staying at home?"

"No, but I certainly could have perished with it," was Premchand's cool reply to such insensitive questions.

He had been writing and teaching for more than a decade, but Premchand was still only a matriculate. Realising he needed at least a graduate degree, he appeared for the pre-university Intermediate exam in English Literature, Persian, Logic and Modern History in March 1916. Despite his poor health and many preoccupations, he managed to pass in the second division. Three years later, he got a B.A. degree from the University of Allahabad.

The bulk of his writing had till then been in Urdu. Now he became more inclined to write in Hindi, in which greater and better-paying opportunities were presenting themselves.

In August 1916, Premchand was transferred again, this time to Gorakhpur, as the Second Master at the Normal School there. It was the same Gorakhpur where he had spent some of the bitter-sweet years of his boyhood.

Premchand reached Gorakhpur with his wife and three year old daughter Kamala on the evening of the 18th of August. The house allotted to them was to be vacated the following day. They were to spend the night of the 18th within the school premises where a crowd of teachers and students welcomed them. Shivarani Devi was pregnant. At about 8 p.m. she felt uneasy. A kind colleague took Premchand's family to his own home where a couple of

No. 968

University of Allahabad.

Intermediate Examination, 1916.

Roll No. 2279 Enrolment No. 1293B

I certify that Dhanpat Rai of Teacher, Basti, College: — passed the Intermediate Examination, held in the month of March, 1916, and was placed in the Second Division.

The subjects in which he was examined were English Literature, Logic Deductive & Inductive ~~or Physiology~~, Classical Language (Persian) & History (Modern) ~~for Mathematics, Biology, Physics and Chemistry.~~

University of Allahabad:
The 5th June, 1916.

M.G.V.Co
Registrar.

Intermediate Examination certificate

hours later Dhunnu (Premchand's elder son Sripat) was born. Premchand was overwhelmed by the affection and help he and his family received from the teachers as well as the Headmaster of the Normal School. Shri Bechan Lal was the absolute opposite of the curt and unhelpful Headmaster in Basti.

Premchand's daily routine was to get up before sunrise and go for an hour's walk within the huge grounds of the school. He then attended to some domestic chores, made his own bed and washed his own clothes, and devoted himself to his writing until it was time to leave for school. He was a stickler for punctuality.

"Premchand came to school usually with his head uncovered, his hair dishevelled, wearing a *dhoti* and a coat which was often unbuttoned. He thus made quite a picture!" recalled one of his students. "We respected him more than we respected anyone else. He taught my class History. Often he would read a passage from the textbook and then cite evidence from other sources to controvert the given version. He would point out that several episodes in the book had been included merely to create divisions between the Hindus and the Muslims... And then before the bell rang, he would clarify that all he had said was for our personal benefit and not to be reproduced in the exams, unless we wanted to fail!"

A year after he joined, Premchand was also appointed superintendent of the school boarding house, bringing his salary to eighty-five rupees a month. He was a popular and successful superintendent being just, impartial and very approachable. About one-fifth of the students at the Normal School were Muslims at that time. There was not a single incident of disharmony between them and the Hindu students. "If ever anyone did something which might provoke communal sentiments, Premchand not only put down the incident but endeavoured to eradicate the very basis of such differences. Considerations of high and low, Hindu and Muslim, and untouchability were all anathema to him."

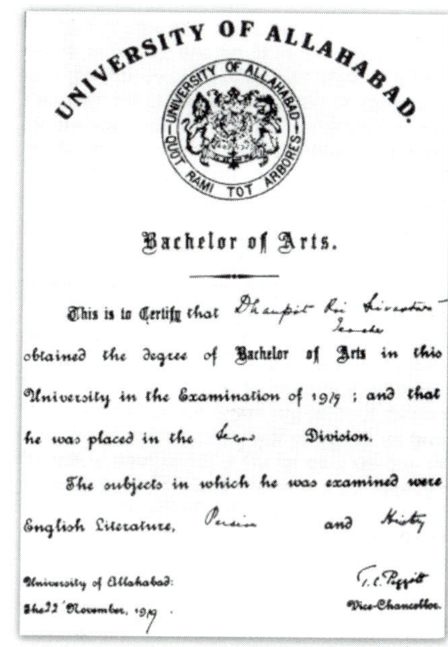

UNIVERSITY OF ALLAHABAD.

UNIVERSITY OF ALLAHABAD — QUOT RAMI TOT ARBORES

Bachelor of Arts.

This is to Certify that Dhanpat Rai Srivastava obtained the degree of Bachelor of Arts in this University in the Examination of 1919; and that he was placed in the Second Division.

The subjects in which he was examined were English Literature, Persian and History

University of Allahabad:
the November, 1919.

Vice-Chancellor.

Certificate of B.A. Examination

On his return from school in the afternoon, Premchand went to the market to buy vegetables and groceries whenever required. He came back to relax in the shade of the mango, neem and jackfruit trees that grew in the open space in front of his house, went through papers, magazines and talked to friends and visitors, his conversation always punctuated by loud laughter. At sunset, he retired to his room to read and write and was in bed by about 10 p.m.

As Premchand began writing in Hindi with greater proficiency and confidence, Hindi journals like *Saraswati* of Allahabad and *Pratap* of Kanpur readily published his stories. Many stories appeared simultaneously in Hindi and Urdu. For the Urdu journal *Zamana*, Premchand had written on some of the masterpieces of Sanskrit and Hindi literature. He now introduced his Hindi readers to the life and work of the famous Persian writer Sheikh Saadi, through a ninety-page booklet entitled *Mahatma Sheikh Saadi.*

The demand and payment for Premchand's stories in Urdu also increased as new journals, such as Imtiaz Ali Taj's *Kahkashan* published from Lahore, made their appearance. Each story now fetched Premchand ten to fifteen rupees. Probably the highest payment was made by Maulana Mohammed Ali. For each story of Premchand's published in his journal *Hamdard*, the Maulana sent the author a gold sovereign, neatly packed, by registered post.

In January 1917, Premchand started work on his next novel. Although *Bazar-e-Husn* (A Beauty of the Market-place), was written originally in Urdu, it was his Hindi version of the novel, entitled *Sevasadan* (The House of Charity), which was published first and did very well. A Gujarati translation also appeared before the Urdu original was published in 1920.

Sevasadan highlighted, among other social problems, the exploitation of women in red-light districts. Premchand's handling of the theme was maturer and the sweep of the novel wider than in his earlier novels.

Mahatma Gandhi

His years in Gorakhpur were the years of Mahatma Gandhi's return to India from South Africa. Premchand followed closely the activties of this new leader who was so utterly different from usual armchair politicians. Like Gandhi, Premchand too had been influenced by the moral tales of the Russian writer Tolstoy, twenty three of which he had adapted to the Indian context. Gandhi's ideals of truth, non-violence and renunciation were the ideals he too held dear and which inspired some of his best work, such as the short story

Panch Parmeshwar, published in 1916.

After finishing *Bazar-e-Husn*, Premchand began writing *Gosha-e-Aafiyat* (A Quiet Corner), the Urdu version of the novel published in Hindi as *Premashram*. This novel of the oppressed and exploited Indian peasant was inspired by Gandhian ideals and by reports of the revolution in Russia. Elsewhere Premchand wrote, "The future belongs to the peasants and workers… India cannot remain unaffected by these winds of change… Who had suspected before the Revolution the tremendous might of the exploited peoples of Russia?"

Leo Tolstoy

The First World War ended in November 1918 and victory celebrations were held all over the country. Premchand did not join the celebration in Gorakhpur. The victory was Britain's, he felt, not India's. The British Director of Education demanded an explanation for Premchand's behaviour from the Headmaster Bechan Lal. Premchand was ready to make a written

The Revolution in Russia, painting by M. Klionski

statement, but Bechan Lal managed to hush up the matter, not wanting Premchand to lose his job.

On another occasion, a visiting British Inspector of Schools drove past Premchand's house in his car. He expected Premchand to get up and *salaam* him. Premchand continued to sit and read on his verandah. The Inspector stopped the car and sent for him.

"This is insolence!" said the Inspector. "Your superior officer passes in front of your house and you can't even get up to greet him."

"I am your subordinate only in school," Premchand said calmly.

"In my own house I am the lord and master."

The Inspector left. Premchand wanted to sue him for defamation. His friends persuaded him not to, but the incident disturbed him for a long time.

It was becoming intolerable for Premchand to continue working for the British Government. But all his attempts to get a teaching job in a private institution were unsuccessful. He toyed with the idea of starting his own newspaper and his own printing press. But how? Where were the resources?

Premchand's second son Munnu had been born in 1919. Eleven months later he died of smallpox. Both husband and wife were devastated, though Premchand remained outwardly calm. Shortly afterwards he himself fell ill. The old complaint, dysentery, returned.

Gandhi was then touring the country to mobilise support for his Non-Cooperation Movement. He came to Gorakhpur on February 8, 1921 to address a crowd of more than two lakh people. Despite ill-health, Premchand was part of the crowd along with his wife and two children.

After hearing Gandhi speak, many months of indecision came to an end for Premchand. He decided to quit government service

provided Shivarani Devi concurred with his decision. She asked for a couple of days to think things over. In view of her husband's failing health, their family responsibilities and meagre resources, it was not easy to consider giving up a secure government job. Then she recalled "how Premchand had recently been so ill that they had given up all hope. He had called her, in effect to say farewell, handing over to her his entire savings of three thousand rupees. If he had then recovered, it must be because God had willed some good to come out of it..."

She supported his decision to resign. On February 15, 1921, Premchand resigned after a little over two decades of government service. Many of his students wanted to quit along with him, but he managed to dissuade them. A few did however leave, out of their attachment to him.

Chapter Four

Freedom to Write

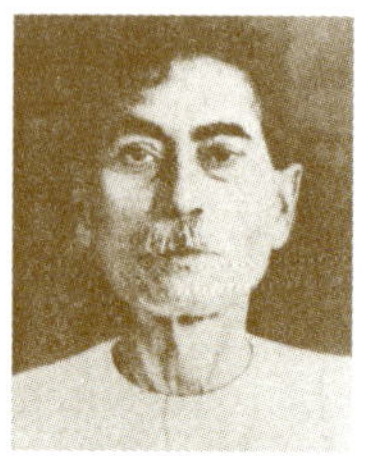

The first story Premchand wrote after quitting government service was *Vichitra Holi* in which the servants of a white man celebrate Holi with great gusto in the *sahib's* own dining room! The story probably reflected the light-heartedness and feeling of victory that Premchand was then experiencing. He continued to write prolifically — stories, articles, pamphlets, becoming, as it were, 'a propagandist of the national Non-Cooperation Movement.'

For a month, he struggled to start a business, selling spinning wheels, but then returned to what he did best — writing. A proposal

that he bring out an Urdu weekly did not work out. In March 1921, Premchand left Gorakhpur for Benaras. He remained keen to start his own paper and, if possible, to buy a printing press. But neither plan materialised. In need of a regular income, he shifted in June to Kanpur as Headmaster of the Marwari School there. His younger son Amrit, nicknamed Bannu, was born in August that year.

Premchand's stint in Kanpur lasted only eight months. He did not see eye to eye with the manager of the school and finally decided to resign. He was back in Benaras in February 1922 and was almost immediately appointed acting editor of a Hindi monthly magazine *Maryada.* He commuted daily from Lamahi where he had begun getting his ancestral home renovated and enlarged. The editorship of *Maryada* ended in July 1922 and Premchand was appointed Headmaster of the Kashi Vidyapeeth School, one of the recently established nationalist institutions of education. This job lasted a year.

The house renovated by Premchand

On July 20, 1923, Premchand fulfilled his dream of starting his own printing press named *Saraswati*, from rented premises in Benaras. From the beginning it was a precarious venture. Premchand had spent all his capital in just setting up the press. He had to borrow from friends like Dayanarayan Nigam to pay for its running expenses. One among such small enterprises, the press could not find much work. Within a year, far from making profit, it lost six hundred rupees.

There was better news on the writing front. Premchand's Hindi novel *Premashram* (The Abode of Love) sold very well. His first play in Hindi — *Sangram* (The Battle), was published in February 1923 and he was able to start work on his next novel *Chaugan-e-Hasti* (The Game of Life) in Urdu. The Hindi version of this novel was called *Rangabhumi* (The Stage).

In an immensely powerful portrayal, Premchand created the hero of *Rangabhumi*, the blind beggar Surdas, "out of his own heart's blood. Surdas is the ideal *satyagrahi*, not merely in the limited political sense but in the wider context of eternal values such as kindness, forgiveness, humility, renunciation, a fearless faith in truth and opposition to injustice — all of which had their origins in the character of Premchand himself, while they also connected him through Tolstoy to Gandhi."

With Jaishankar Prasad

In September 1924, Premchand moved with his family to Lucknow for a

Still from Satyajit Ray's film based on Premchand's short story Shatranj Ke Khiladi

year, as literary advisor to the Ganga Pustakmala Publishing House, on a salary of one hundred rupees a month. The Saraswati Press did not provide him with a steady, sufficient income, hence the necessity for yet another move.

In Lucknow, Premchand stayed healthy and continued to write prolifically. The beautifully ironic study of honour and decadence — his famous short story *Shatranj Ke Khiladi* (The Chess Players), was written during this period.

He usually wrote sitting on the floor, before a small sloping desk, impervious to the din his children made around him. Visitors, including aspiring writers whom he always guided, came at all hours. Premchand refused to regulate this flow. "I can't turn myself into a *Burra Sahib*," he said. "If anyone comes to see me, he is being kind to me. I can't reject or slight him. As for my work, it is an integral part of my life. It will go on anyhow." As soon as his visitor left, he resumed writing.

He completed the novel he had begun after *Rangabhumi*. Entitled *Kayakalp* (The Metamorphosis), it was a study of society torn apart by communal tension, injustice and exploitation. What he depicted was the reality he saw around him. Hindu and Muslim fanatics were baying for each other's blood. In hard-hitting articles, in stories like *Bauram*, *Muktidhan* and *Mandir aur Masjid*, and in a play called *Karbala*, Premchand strove to restore fellow feeling in the two warring communities.

Premchand : 1925

The play offended some Muslim hardliners, just as his earlier article criticising the 'purification' of Muslims at the hands of Hindus, had offended some Hindus. There were long delays before both the play and the article were published. Meanwhile Premchand continued to write undeterred. He also managed to keep his sense of humour intact. When a Hindu journalist declared that Muslims who committed atrocities deserved tit-for-tat treatment, Premchand gently advocated restraint.

"Sir," said the journalist, "if a man started piddling right in front of you, what would you do?"

"Move away a little," said Premchand.

"And if he confronted you and repeated the act?"

"I would move away again."

"And if he came after you and again did the same thing?"

"Sir," asked the amused but exasperated Premchand, "are we talking about a man or a water sprinkler?"

Premchand returned to Benaras in September 1925. From November, his new novel *Nirmala* was serialised in the Hindi magazine *Chand* and published as a book in 1927. It was a heartrending story of the plight of young girl married to a much older man and it proved immensely popular. Its serialisation was followed by that of *Pratigya*, a maturer version of Premchand's twenty-year-old novel *Prema*.

On February 15, 1927, Premchand was back in Lucknow, this time as editor of the Hindi magazine *Madhuri*, on a salary of two hundred rupees a month. Unrelated work like preparing text books for the Nawal Kishore Press which published *Madhuri*, and getting the textbooks prescribed, was also thrust upon him. Despite the extra burden, recalled a Muslim colleague, "I always found him cheerful.... His laughter used to fill the room and spread a kind of radiance.... Once I narrated to him an anecdote about a *muezzin* who called the faithful to prayer even as he himself kept running away from the mosque. Asked what he was up to, he replied that he wanted to hear how his call sounded from afar! Premchand laughed so much at this anecdote that tears came to his eyes."

The Simon Commission landed in India in February 1928 and the entire country rose in revolt. Ironically, during this turbulent period, Premchand was offered the title of Rai Bahadur by the British Government. Very politely he declined it. Recognition of his talent as a writer also came from other unexpected quarters. His stories

Premchand, with family

began to be translated into English and then into German and Japanese.

"I hardly need to say that you are the greatest Hindi writer of the modern age," wrote the Professor of Hindi at the University of Berlin, in a letter to Premchand.

In March 1930, Premchand fulfilled another long-cherished dream by launching his own literary-political monthly *Hans* (the Swan) — the mythological vehicle of the Goddess of Knowledge, Saraswati. January 26, 1930 had been declared *Poorna Swarajya* (full independence) Day, with the entire nation pledging itself to the goal of total independence. 1930 witnessed tremendous clashes with the British Government. Through *Hans*, Premchand spoke out fearlessly against the government's policy of repression. He was penalised by a demand of one thousand rupees as security from his press. This forced him to close down both the magazine and the press for four months until the Press Ordinance was lifted.

Premchand's house was next door to the Congress office, the hub of nationalist activity. Right in front of the house was Aminuddaula Park where public meetings were regularly held, illicit salt made and bonfires lit of foreign-made cloth. Premchand and Shivarani Devi sent off many *satyagrahis* with a *tilak* on their foreheads.

Inspired and feeling perhaps freer after the marriage of her daughter Kamala, Shivarani Devi quietly joined the freedom movement, without letting her husband know. Like him, she had not been keeping too well and feared that he might stop her for that reason. In July she was arrested while picketing a shop selling foreign cloth and was sentenced to two months' imprisonment.

"I was planning to go to jail myself," wrote Premchand to a good friend and fellow writer Jainendra Kumar. "But she beat me to it and barred my way." On her return, Shivarani Devi was embarrassed to find that Premchand had hung a photograph of her on the wall

Premchand, Rishabhcharan and Jainendrakumar

in his room, and garlanded it with flowers and sandalwood!

The proprieter of the Nawal Kishore Press died suddenly in early 1931. The management changed hands and not quite seeing eye to eye with it, Premchand decided to quit his job and return to Benaras. The progress of his own press had been erratic. To make matters worse, in August 1932, the security on *Hans* was reimposed.

Despite his precarious financial condition, Premchand could not resist the temptation to take over and run another magazine — the weekly *Jagaran* (Awakening). In *Jagaran's* inaugural issue he wrote, "The goal of this publication will be a search for the truth.... It will oppose injustice regardless of whether the offender is a king or society or religion.... It will laugh and make others laugh.... The man who never laughs out loud is only half alive...."

He concluded his manifesto with a dig at himself.

"We have neither the organisation nor the experience. As for money, we have an ancestral estrangement with it!"

Hans had just restarted after four months when the government demanded a security of two thousand rupees from *Jagaran* and the Saraswati Press. Once again Premchand had to run from pillar to post for succour.

"One need only breathe," he wrote to Jainendra Kumar, "to find a knife at one's throat."

Taken on with such enthusiasm, *Jagaran* unfortunately never proved to be financially viable, forcing him to close it down within two years. Both magazines and the press were, for several reasons, a continual drain on his meagre resources.

"It was an evil day on which I started the press," he wrote bitterly to Jainendra Kumar in February 1934, "Ten thousand rupees and eleven years of hard work and hassles — all down the drain. How many friends have I estranged, with how many have I broken my word, and how much valuable time have I wasted in correcting proofs instead of using it for my own reading and writing — all for the sake of this press. This has been the greatest blunder of my life!"

In an attempt to undo this blunder, Premchand accepted an offer from a film company in Bombay. For eight thousand rupees a year, he was to write four or five scenarios for the company, being free to write and publish whatever else he wanted. His fifteen-year-old novel *Sevasadan* was already being made into a film.

Premchand moved to Bombay in May 1934. Shivarani Devi joined him in July, after settling the two boys in Allahabad. The Bombay

Premchand signing a contract with Ajanta Cinetone

experience was in no way a happy or satisfying one for Premchand. His views and those of the film producers were poles apart. He was asked to flesh out a melodramatic plot for the film *Mazdoor*. The film was opposed by Bombay's mill owners, censored and finally banned by the government, after crowds of mill workers thronged cinema houses where it was shown.

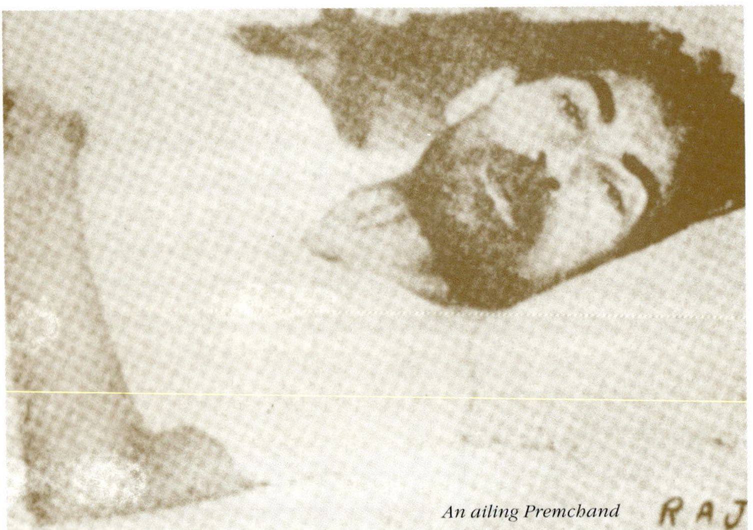

An ailing Premchand

Adding to Premchand's frustrations, the Saraswati Press workers in Benaras went on strike. Premchand was deeply hurt. He had carried on with a loss, making press largely to safeguard their interests. However the strike soon ended and the workers returned to their jobs.

Premchand returned to Benaras in April 1935, three months before the expiry of his contract and giving up two thousand rupees due to him. The film company was winding up and he did not want to add to their problems.

"The cinema is not the right place for a literary person," he wrote to a friend, "and I am returning to literature again."

M.S. Subbulakshmi as 'Suman' in the Tamil film based on Premchand's novel 'Sevasadan'

Taking into account all his expenses, Premchand returned home "richer by just fourteen hundred rupees and a lot wiser."

His precarious health had worsened in Bombay. But nothing could stop him from working, often late into the night. An angry and worried Shivarani Devi would snatch away his pen. But the moment her back was turned, he would resume writing.

"I am making no sacrifices Rani," he said. "I do this because I want to do it. So long as there is oil in a lamp, it does its duty. When the oil finishes, the lamp goes out...."

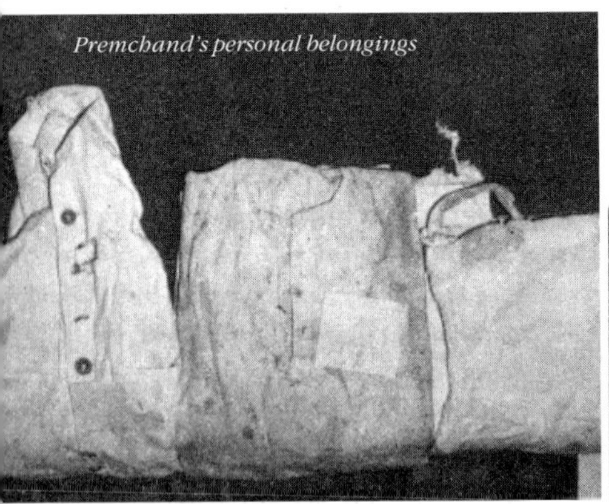

Premchand's personal belongings

His spectacles and suitcase

That summer in Lamahi he finished writing his last complete novel *Godan* (The Gift of a Cow). This time the portrayal of social injustice, back-breaking poverty and human misery was unsparing. Unlike some of his earlier novels, in *Godan* there are no easy answers, no compromises with reality. And yet the darkness is illumined by a new serenity, a mature acceptance of life in all its shades. Usually stoic, Shivarani Devi could not hold back her tears when she read *Godan*.

For Premchand, social reform had always been as important as political independence. As a character in one of his early stories had said, freedom didn't mean merely 'putting Govind in place of John'. The crying need of the freedom struggle at that stage was

national unity. And for national unity, an integrating language seemed essential to him.

Premchand's wife Shivarani Devi

"You cannot strengthen the roots of your nation without the pivotal support of a national language," Premchand had said in his speech of welcome at the National Language Convention held in Bombay in October 1934. According to him the national language could only be a mixture of Hindi and Urdu-Hindustani, the language of Hindustan, of Hindus as well as Muslims. The stranglehold of English had to be broken.

In December that year, Premchand had also addressed the annual convention of the Hindi Prachar Sabha, Society for the Propagation of Hindi, held in Madras on 'the cause of spreading Hindi in a non-Hindi State.'

He could not attend the annual session of the Hindi Sahitya Sammelan, held in Indore in April 1935 and presided over by Gandhi, in which the need for a national language and a national literary council was discussed. But with Gandhi's approval,

Clockwise — Kamala, Mahtab Rai, Sripat Rai, Amrit Rai

Premchand's magazine *Hans* became the official journal of the Bharatiya Sahitya Parishad (Indian Literary Council).

In January 1936, Premchand presided over the annual comvention of the Nagari Pracharini Sabha, the society for the propagation of Hindi, in Agra. In March 1936, he inaugurated the Hindustani Sabha at the Jamia Millia in New Delhi. "For the first time," he wrote in *Hans*, "Urdu and Hindi writers met to found together a Hindustani Sabha, whose aim will be to bring together writers from both languages, to provide opportunities for them to understand and appreciate the thoughts and sentiments of each other and to organise the development of the Hindustani language."

In April, he was persuaded to preside over the first all-India conference of the recently formed Progressive Writers' Association, in Lucknow.

"We must change our criterion of beauty," he said in his address. "Art has been, and still is, taken to mean a narrow aestheticism. Its view is not yet wide enough to comprehend the sublime beauty of the battle of life.... For it, beauty lies in a lovely woman, but not in that plain, poor mother of many children who has put her baby to sleep at the edge of the field and is now sweating in toil.... This is the defect of a narrow vision.... The Temple of Literature has no

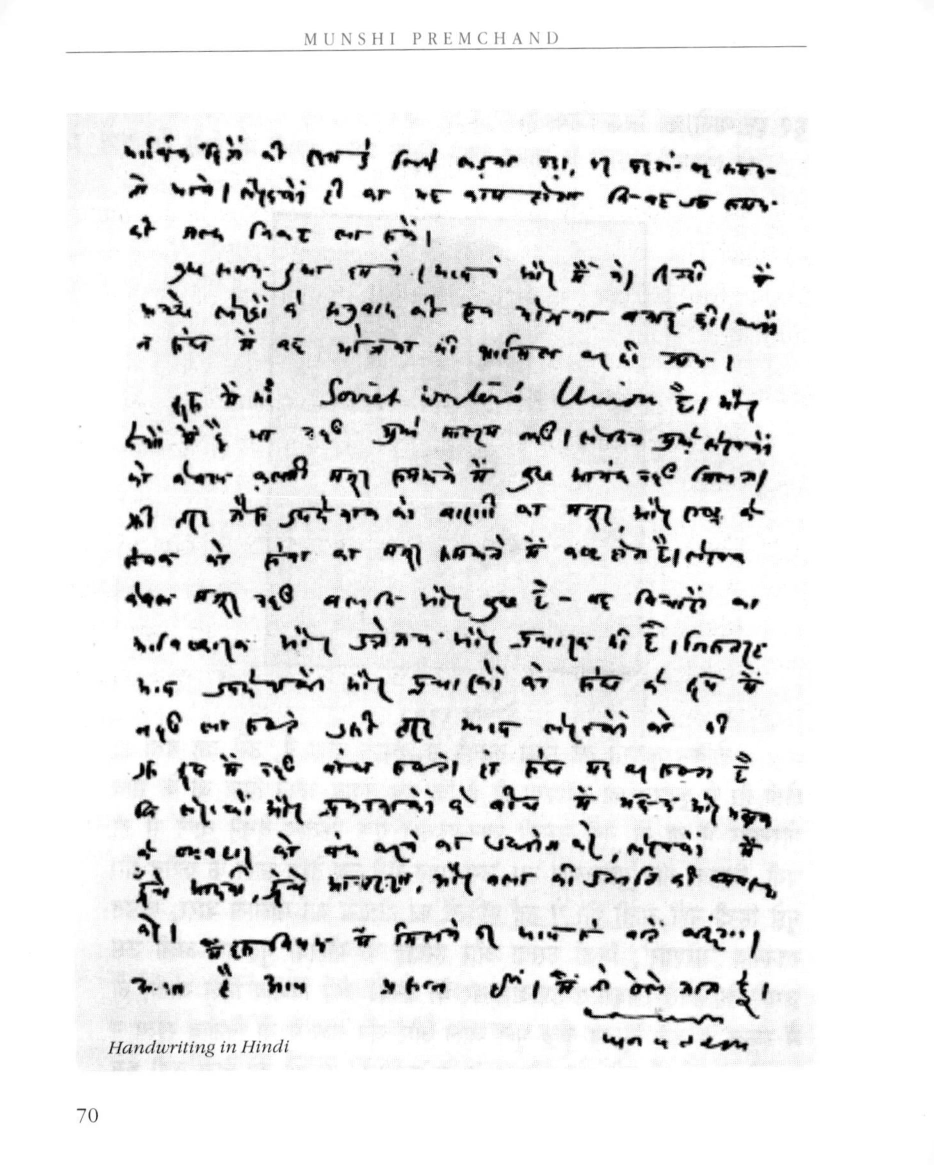

Handwriting in Hindi

place for the devotees of wealth and splendour.... If we serve society with sincerity and devotion; honour, prestige and fame will kiss our feet. Why then should we bother about honour and prestige? The spiritual joy of service should be our true reward.... We are foot-soldiers, marching on with the banner of society in our hands."

Behind each word of Premchand's nearly two hour long address lay a lifetime of commitment and passionate conviction. The packed hall listened in pin-drop silence.

Immediately after the conference, Premchand left for Lahore, where he received a tremendous welcome. It was heartwarming for him to see the extent of his popularity as a writer in Punjab. "He addressed dozens of meetings on the twin themes of the movement for progressive literature, of which he was the recently acclaimed president; and of the Hindustani Sabha of which he was the founder and chief spokesman."

Chapter Five

The Lamp Goes Out

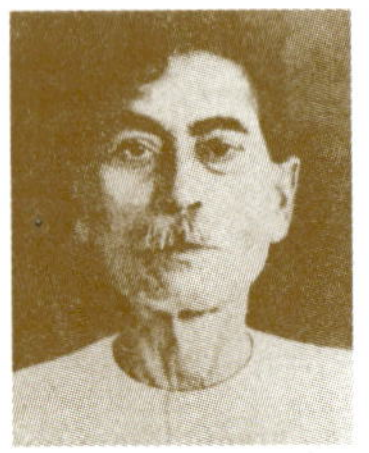

So much travel and hectic activity took its toll. On June 16, 1936 Premchand fell ill. Although he continued to work, he never again had a full meal or a good night's sleep. He was prevailed upon to consult a leading doctor in Lucknow, who diagnosed his condition as advanced cirrhosis of the liver.

"The lamp was going out..." Premchand returned to Benaras 'a mere skeleton, his face grown yellow as old paper, his eyes sunken.' He lay in bed unable to get up or walk. But there was no bitterness, no regret, no railing against fate. 'He had done what he had to do and said what he had to say.'

Premchand died on the morning of October 8, 1936. He was just fifty six years old.

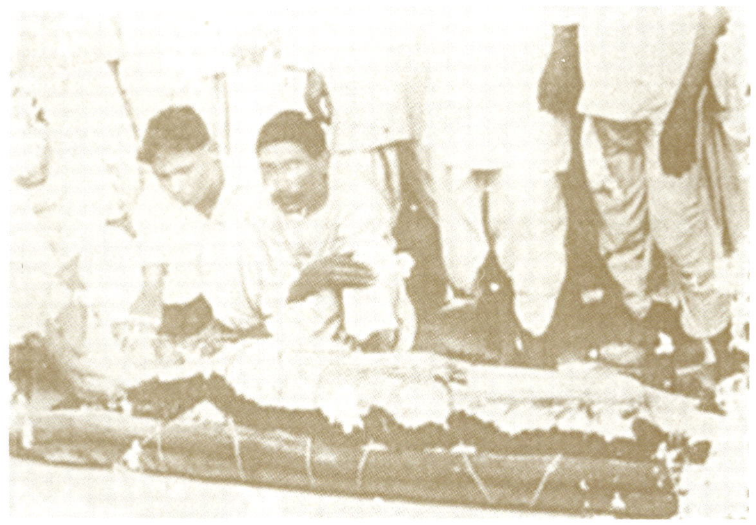

Preparations for his last journey

Underestimating, as many great writers have done, his own genius and its impact on posterity, Premchand once wrote:

"My life is like a stretch of plain and level ground, which has its share of pits and ditches, but has no room for hills, mountains, dense forests, deep valleys or picturesque ruins. Those who would rather climb mountains are bound to be disappointed here."

On this 'plain and level ground', towers the evergreen tree of Premchand's writing; strongly rooted not just in the often harsh and still unchanged realities of Indian society, but in the very bedrock of the human condition.

Strongly rooted, it endures.

Premchand's Novels

In Urdu	***In Hindi***
Asrar-e-Ma'abid	
Bazar-e-Husn	Sevasadan
Chaugan-e-Hasti	Rangabhumi
	Ghaban
Gaudan	Godan
Gosh-e-Aafiyat	Premashram
Humkhurma-o-Hamsawab	Prema
Jalwa-e-Isar	Vardan
Maidan-e-Amal	Karmabhumi
Parda-e-Majaz	Kayakalp
	Kishna
Mangalsutra (unfinished)	
	Nirmala
Bewa	Pratigya

Plays

In Hindi & Urdu

Karbala

Sangram

Short Story Collections

In Hindi & Urdu

Prem Pachisi

Prem Prasoon

In Urdu

Soz-e-Vatan

In Hindi

Mansarovar (8 volumes)

Along with innumerable articles, translations and letters.

भारत
INDIA
30
PREM CHAND 1880-1936
1980

BIBLIOGRAPHY

In Hindi

1. *Premchand — Qalam Ka Sipahi* by Amrit Rai, Hans Prakashan, Allahabad.
2. *Premchand Ghar Mein* by Shivarani Devi Premchand, Atmaram and Sons, Delhi.

In English

1. *Premchand — His Life and Times* by Amrit Rai (Translated by Harish Trivedi) Oxford University Press, New Delhi.
2. *Munshi Premchand — A Literary Biography* by Madan Gopal, Asia Publishing House, India.
3. *Premchand — A Life in Letters* by Jainendra Kumar (Translated by Sunita Jain) Y.K. Publishers, Agra.
4. *Premchand, His Life & Works* by V.S. Naravane, Vikas, Delhi.
5. *Premchand, Novelist & Thinker* by Govind Narain Sharma, Pragati Publications, Delhi.